Vol 5

MAZE

Ages 4-6

FOR KIDS

MAZE BOOK

SOCIAL MEDIA

/MySweetBooks1

/MySweetBooks1

/MySweetBooks1

/MySweetBooks

Email Us : mysweetbooks1@gmail.com

Printed in USA
Published by My Sweet Books

Milk

MILK

Milk

milk

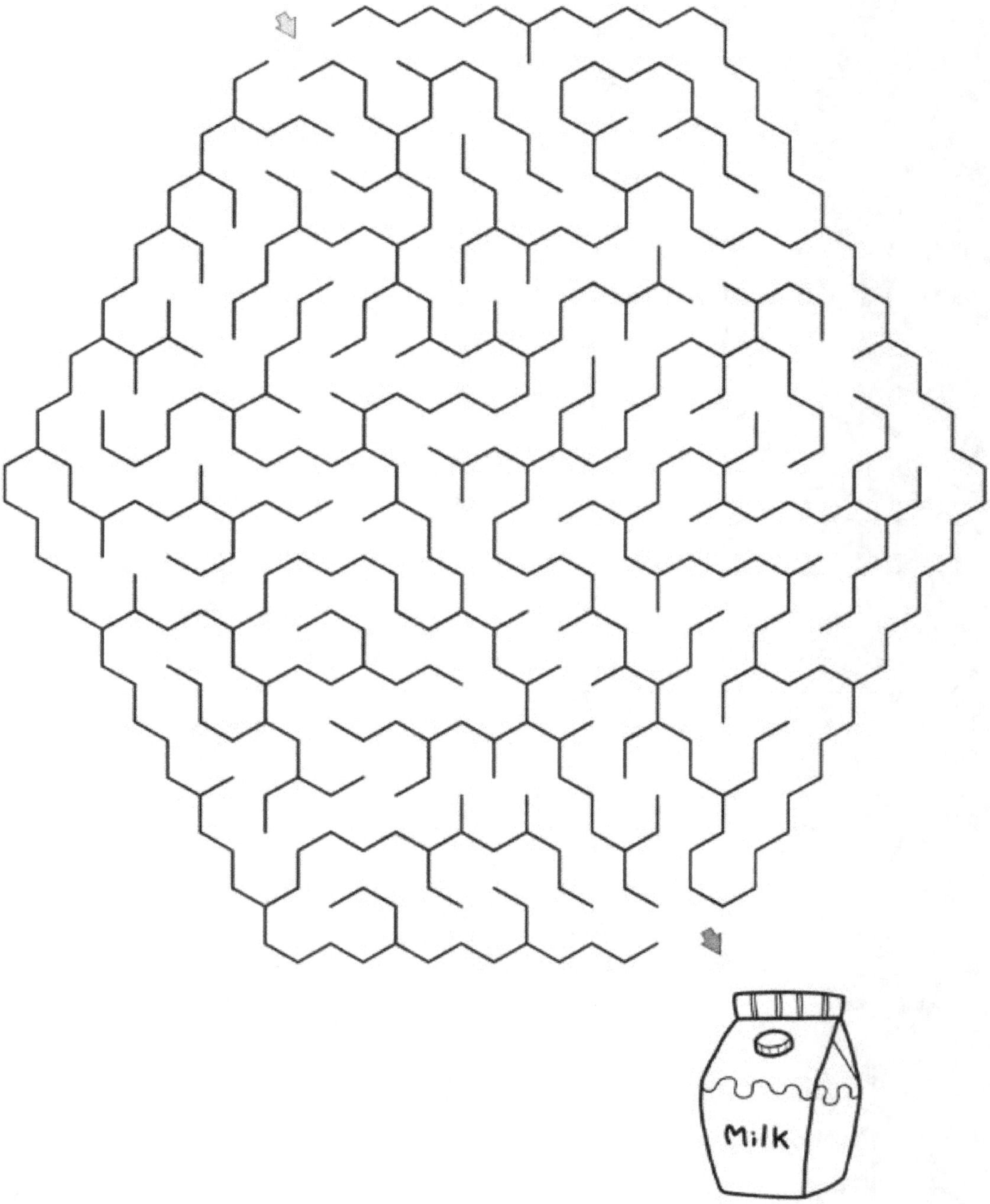

Milk

MILK

Milk

Milk

MILK

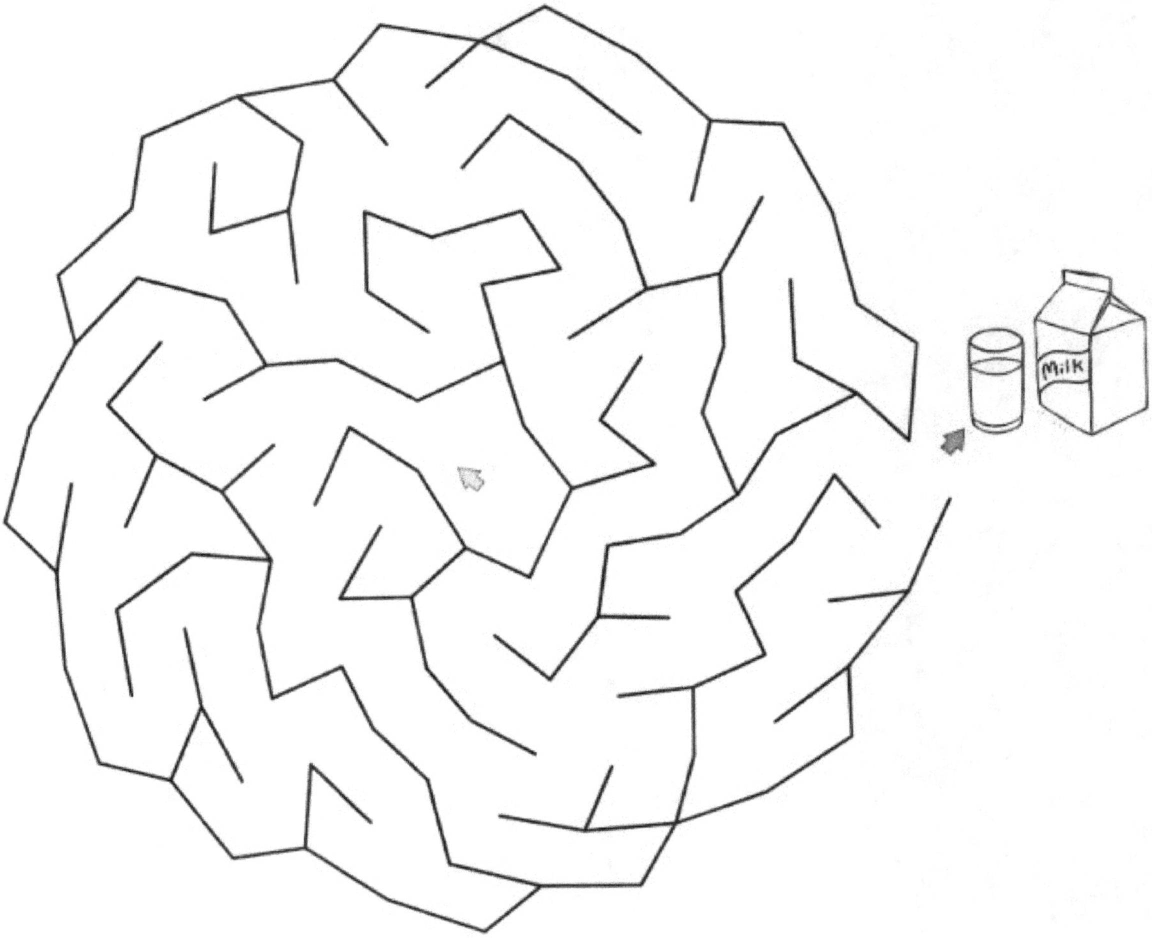
MILK

milk

milk

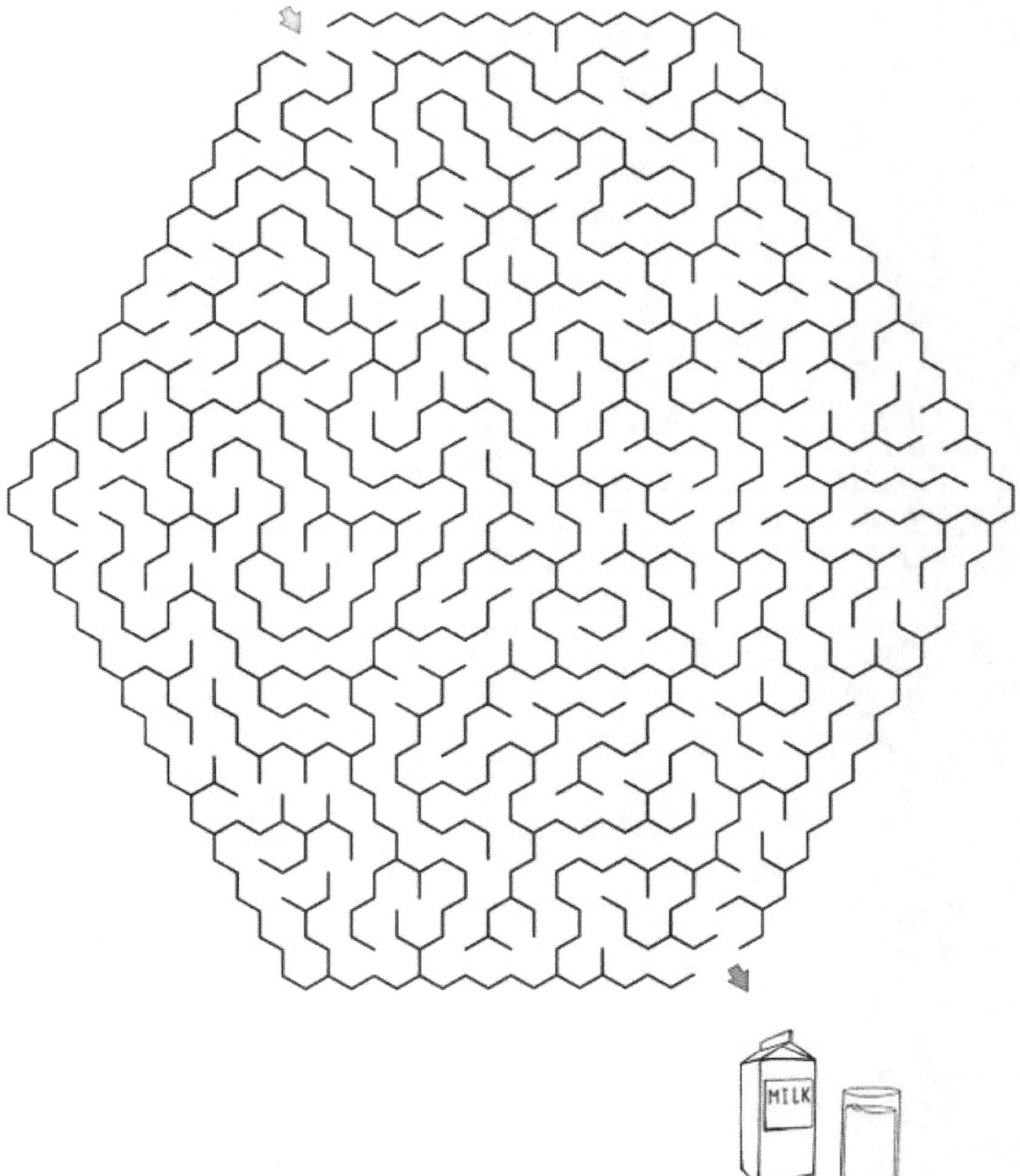
MILK

Milk

Milk

MILK

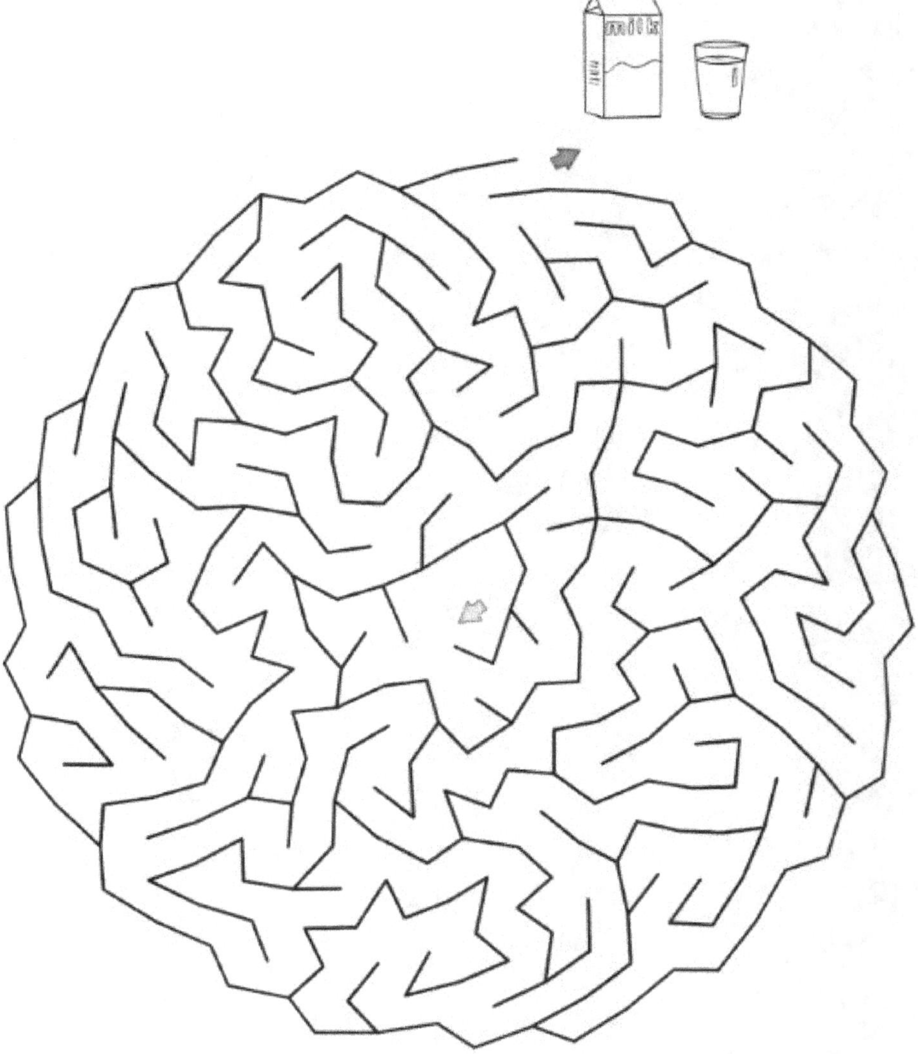
milk

Milk

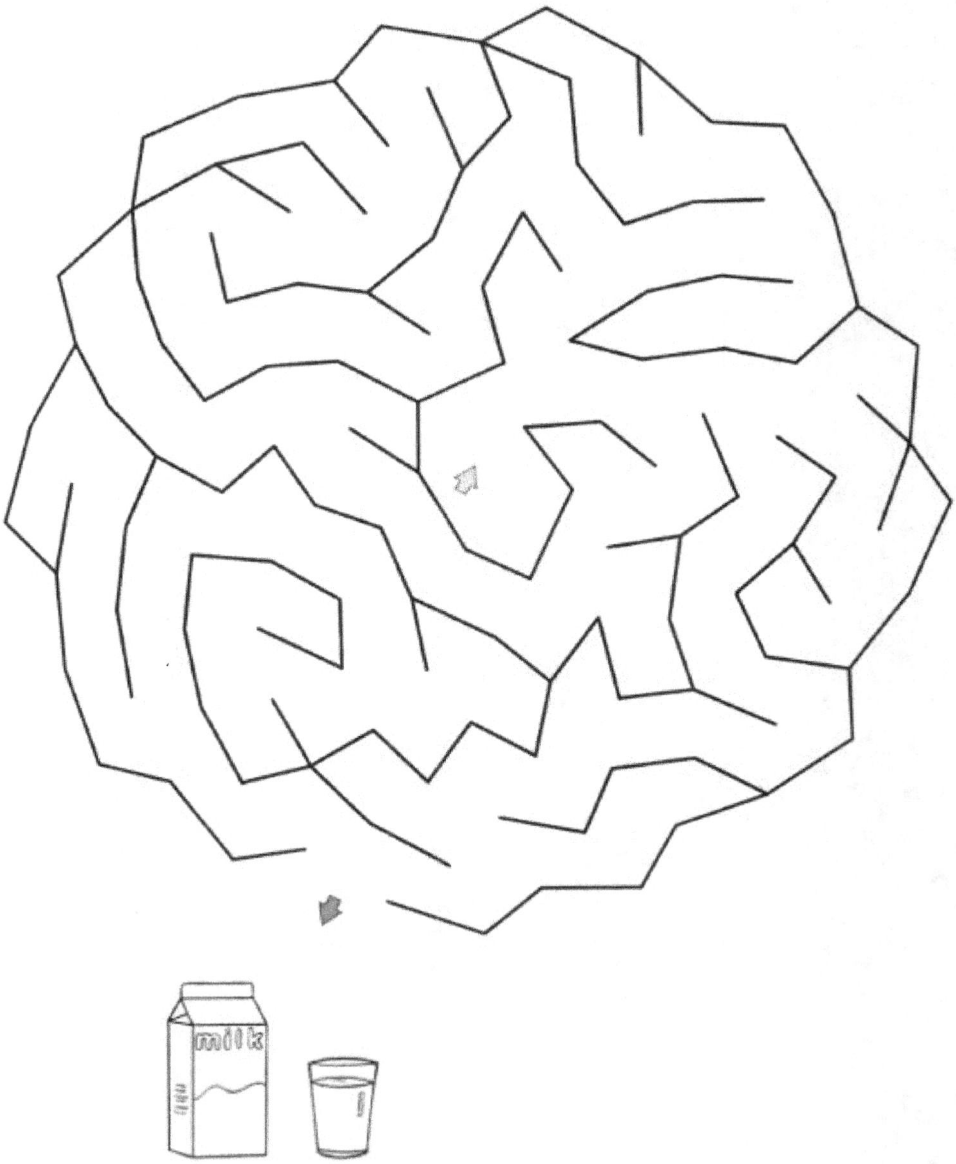
milk

Milk

MILK

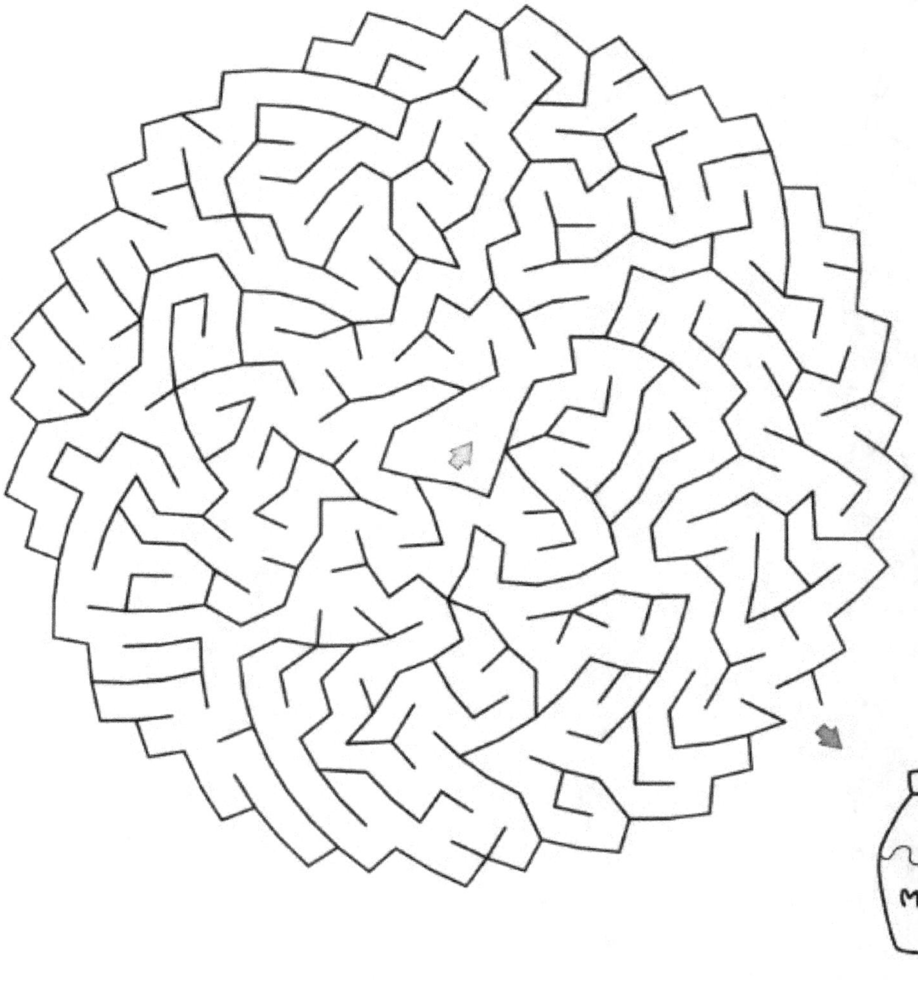
Milk

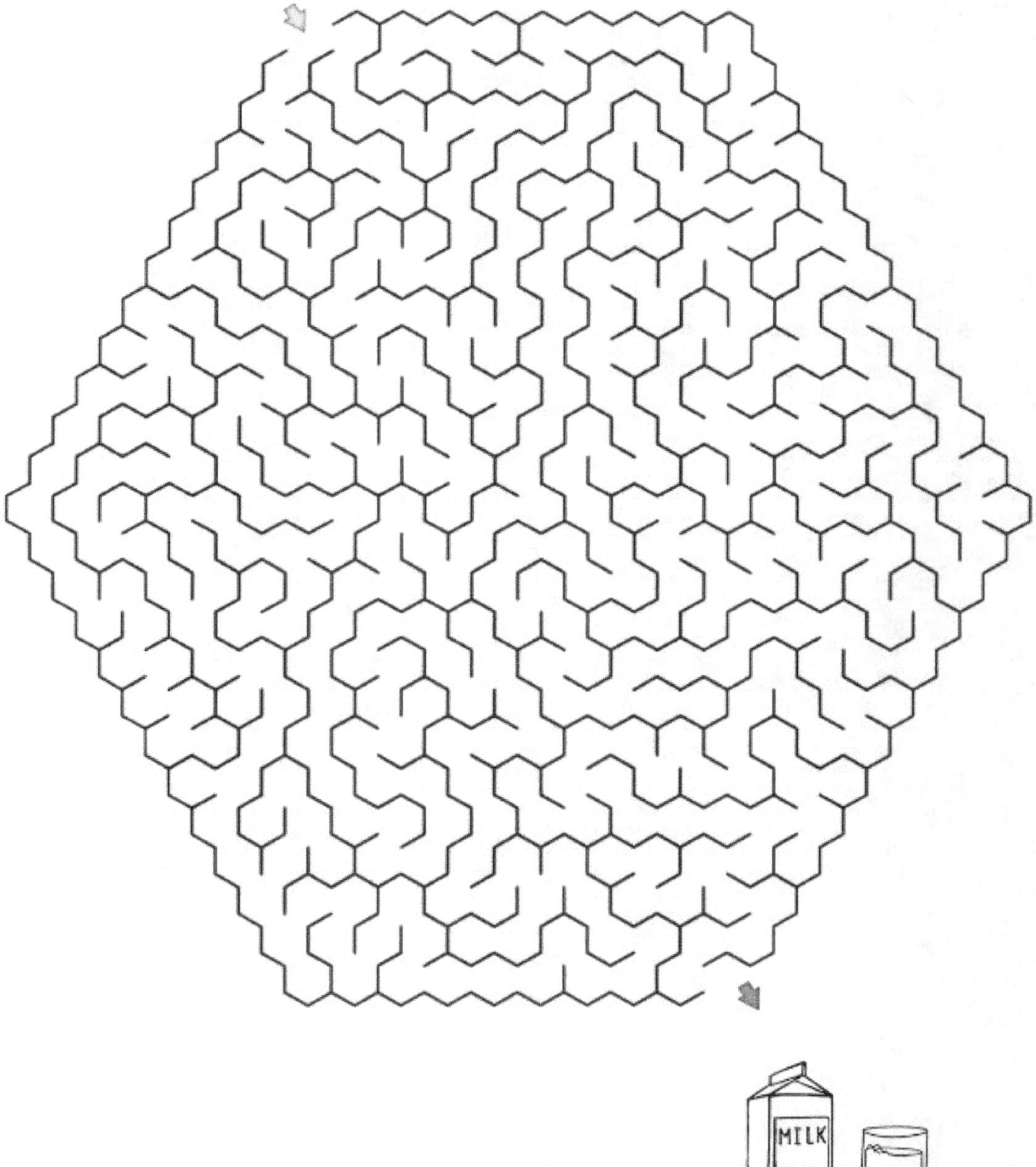
MILK

Milk

milk

Milk

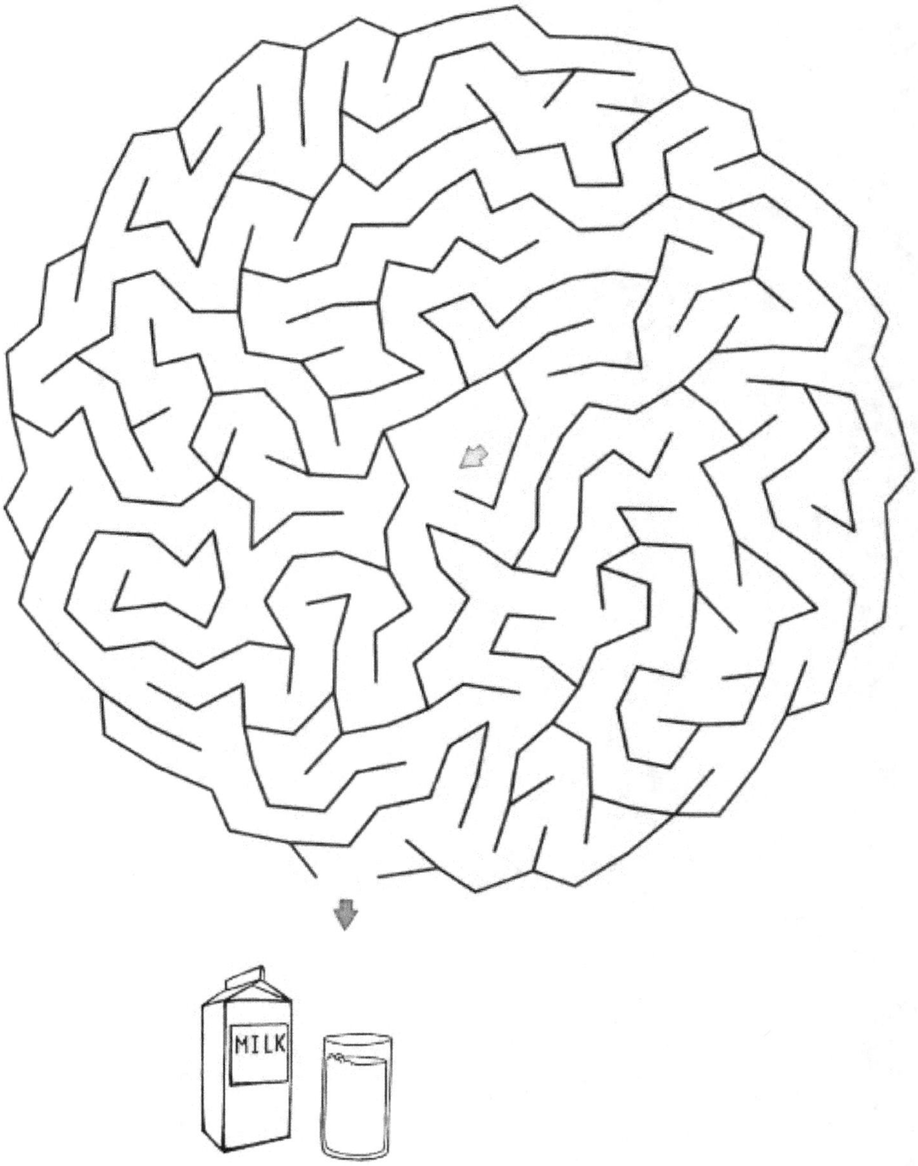
MILK

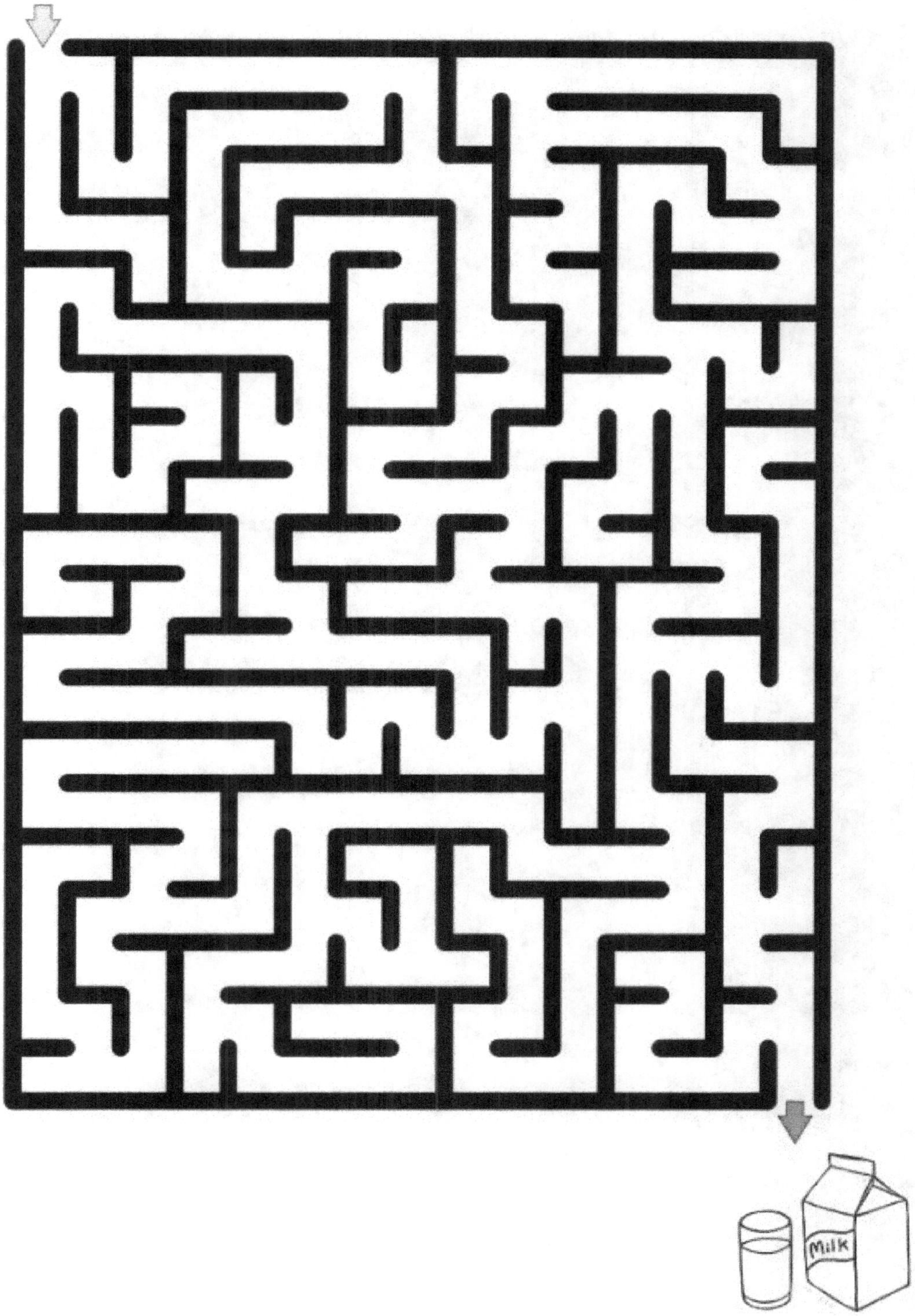
Milk

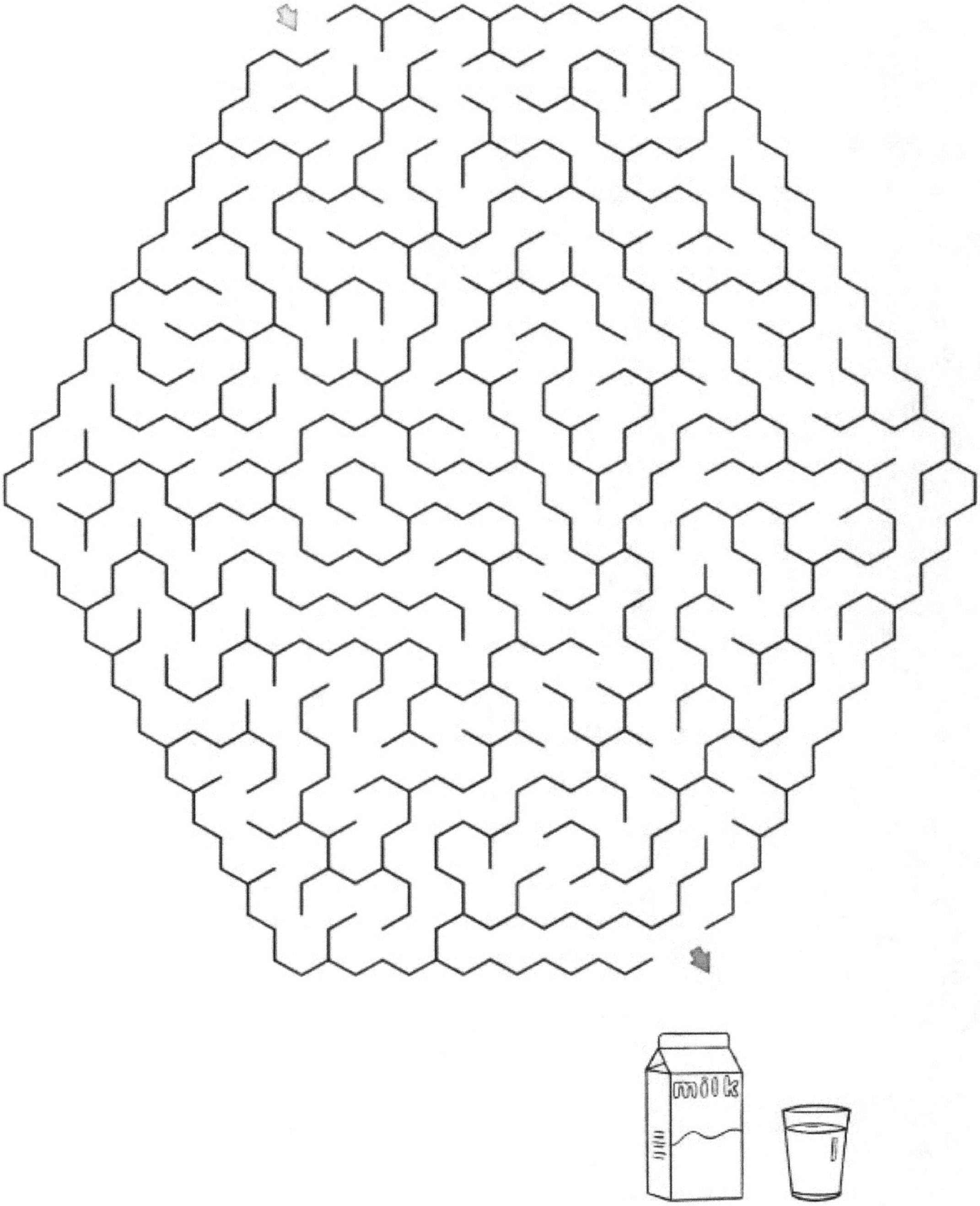
milk

Milk

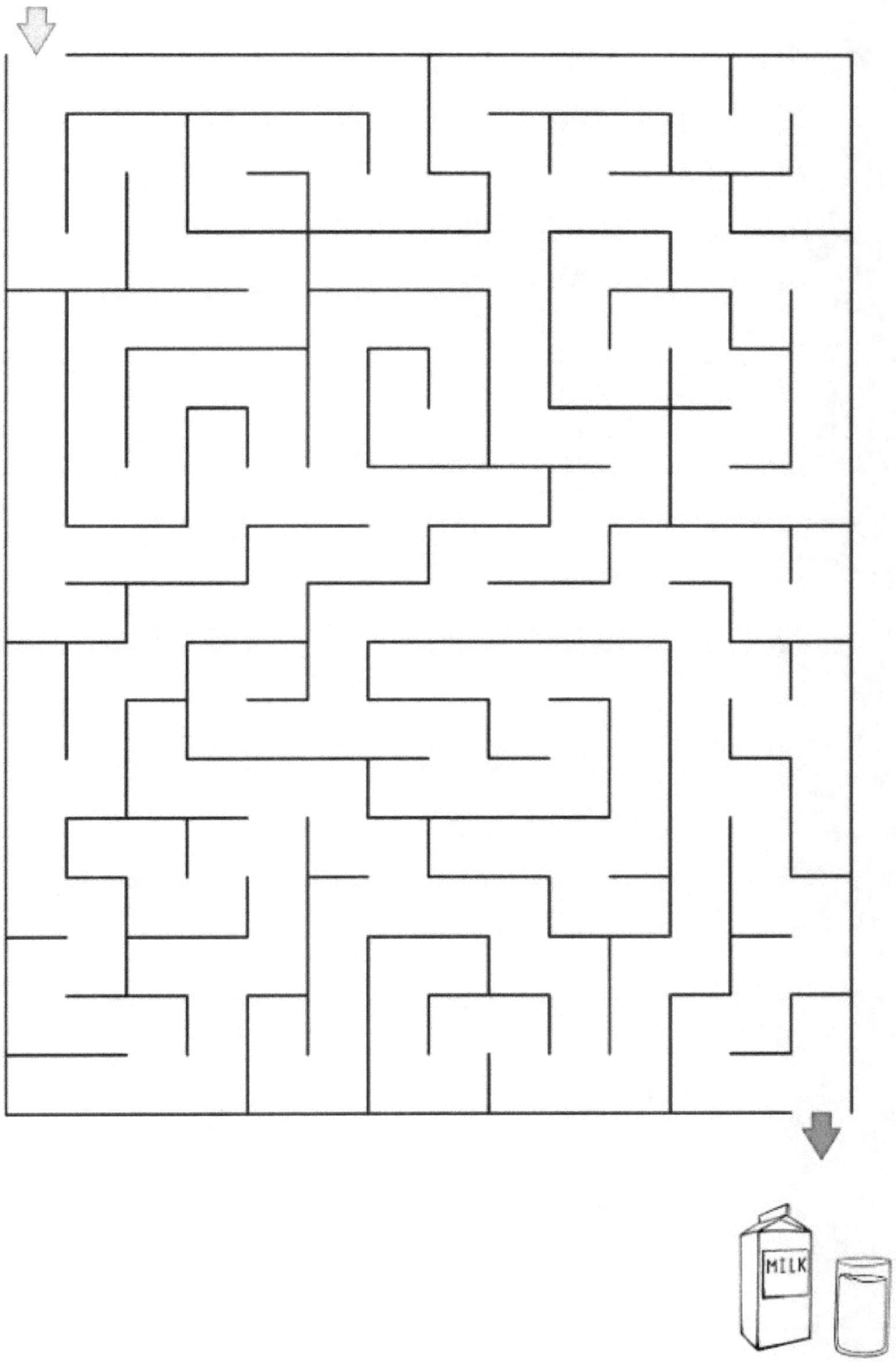
MILK

Milk

milk

Milk

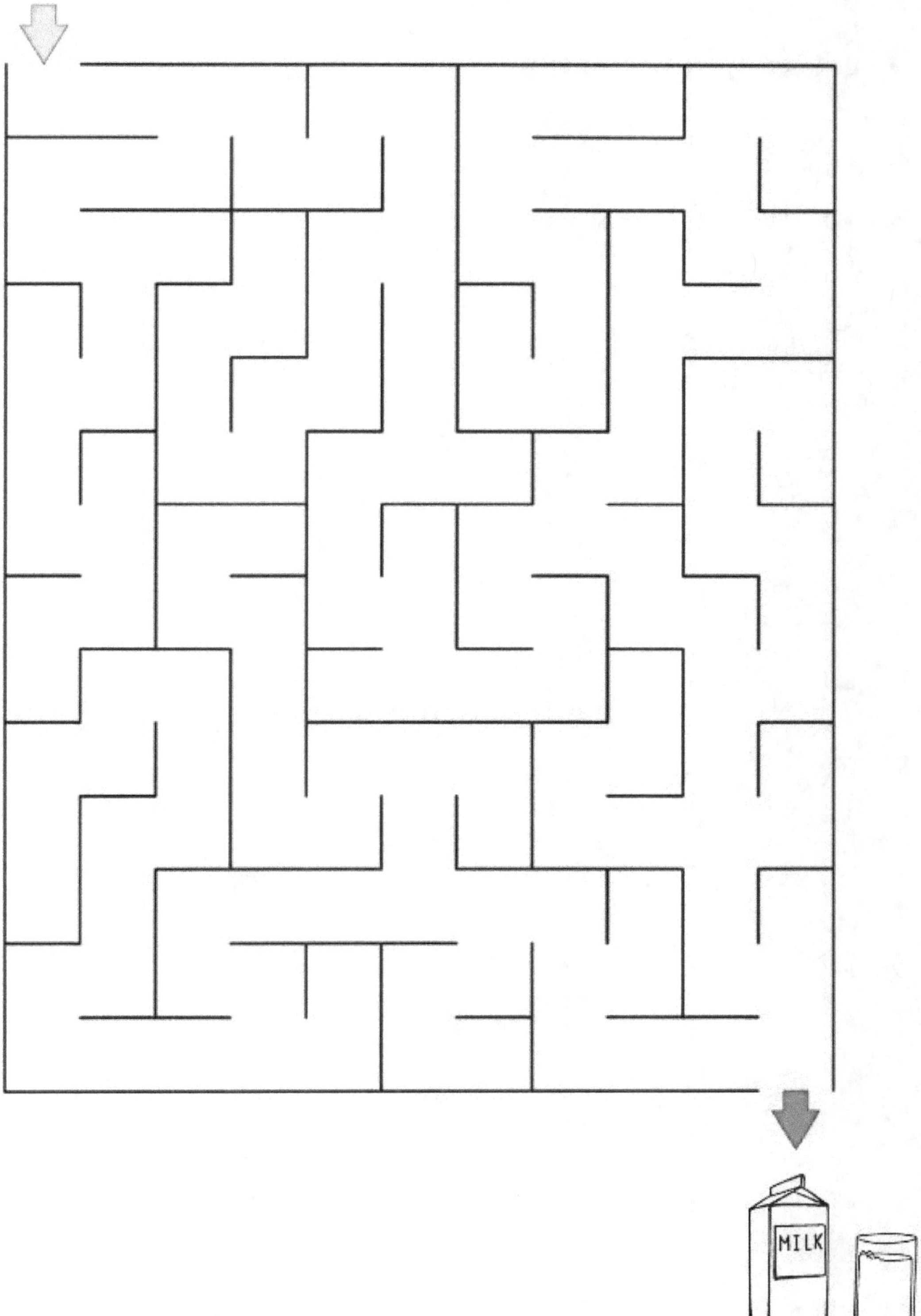
MILK

Milk

milk

Milk

MILK

www.ingramcontent.com/pod-product-compliance
Lightning Source LLC
Chambersburg PA
CBHW081739250726
48657CB00010B/3340
* 9 7 8 1 7 0 4 9 2 8 8 6 9 *